PRENTICE HALL

UNITED STATES HISTORY

All-in-One
Teaching Resources

The Conservative Resurgence (1980–1993)

PEARSON
Prentice
Hall

Upper Saddle River, New Jersey
Boston, Massachusetts

Acknowledgements

Pages 27, 30: From On This Day: 1989: The Night The Wall Came Down. Copyright © BBC

NOTE: Every effort has been made to locate the copyright owner of material reprinted in this book. Omissions brought to our attention will be corrected in subsequent editions.

Upper Saddle River, New Jersey
Boston, Massachusetts

ISBN 0-13-203708-4

1 2 3 4 5 6 7 8 9 10 10 09 08 07 06

Name _____ Class _____ Date _____

Letter Home

Dear Family,

Over the coming weeks, our United States history class will be reading a chapter called The Conservative Resurgence. The following information will give you some background to the content your student will be studying.

During the 1900s, two dominant political parties emerged in the United States. These parties gained members attracted by specific ideologies, or ideas about the ways that society and government should function. The Republican party reflected conservative ideologies, and the Democratic party reflected liberal ideologies. Although both parties believed in a democratic system of government, each interpreted the Constitution differently and envisioned the purpose of government differently. Conservatives tended to view government as an instrument of order, a way to keep society safe, secure, and organized so that individual citizens could work toward individual goals. Liberals tended to view government as a system to provide for the general welfare of all citizens by ensuring equal rights and opportunities.

Many Americans became disillusioned with the predominantly Democratic policies of the mid-1900s. Some people criticized liberal economic policies as failures that led to high inflation and recession in the late 1970s. Others criticized the rise of the counterculture as dangerous to traditional Christian values. Still others resisted the reforms of the civil rights movement. Each of these trends contributed to the rise of a new conservative movement known as the New Right. In 1980, the New Right succeeded in electing Ronald Reagan as President, and altered the balance between the parties in Congress.

President Reagan took the United States in a different direction from previous administrations. Like most conservatives, Reagan favored limited government involvement in the economy. He urged Congress to cut taxes, reduce spending on social programs, and deregulate the banking, telecommunications, and airlines industries. At the same time, Reagan took an aggressive stance toward the Cold War. He pushed massive spending increases through Congress and engaged in a huge military buildup. Unfortunately, these spending increases did not balance with the tax cuts, and the budget deficit and national debt soared. Although economic growth did occur, the gap between the rich and the poor widened, and unemployment surged among farmers and blue-collar workers.

Throughout the 1980s, the United States became involved in conflicts in Latin America and Asia, an involvement that would continue into the next century. When the communist block of the Soviet Union and Eastern Europe collapsed at the end of the decade, people around the world celebrated what they considered a new birth of democracy. The United States became the sole superpower. As such, the nation and its conservative and liberal leaders inherited a new set of economic, political, and military challenges.

In the weeks ahead, your student may wish to share what he or she is learning with you. Please participate in your child's educational experience through discussion and involvement.

Sincerely,

EL RESURGIMIENTO DEL CONSERVADURISMO
Carta para el hogar

Estimada familia,

En las próximas semanas, nuestra clase de historia de Estados Unidos va a leer un capítulo llamado "El resurgimiento del conservadurismo". La siguiente información le dará a usted algunos conocimientos sobre el tema que su estudiante va a estudiar.

Durante el siglo XX, dos partidos políticos dominantes emergieron en Estados Unidos. Estos partidos atrajeron miembros por medio de dos ideologías específicas o ideas acerca de las maneras en que la sociedad y el gobierno debían funcionar. El partido Republicano reflejó las ideologías conservadoras y el partido Demócrata reflejó las ideologías liberales. Aunque ambos partidos creían en un sistema democrático de gobierno, cada uno interpretaba la Constitución de manera diferente y tenían una visión diferente del propósito del gobierno. Los conservadores tendían a ver al gobierno como un instrumento del orden, una manera de mantener segura y organizada a la sociedad de modo que los ciudadanos pudieran trabajar hacia metas individuales. Los liberales tendían a ver al gobierno como un sistema que proporcionara el bienestar general para todos los ciudadanos, asegurando igualdad de derechos y oportunidades.

Muchos estadounidenses se decepcionaron con las políticas predominantemente democráticas de mediados del siglo XX. Algunas personas criticaban las políticas económicas como fallidas y que habían llevado a una alta inflación y una recesión a fines de la década de 1970. Otros criticaban el aumento de una contracultura como peligrosa para los valores cristianos tradicionales. Incluso otros se resistían a las reformas del movimiento por los derechos civiles. Cada una de estas tendencias contribuyó al surgimiento de un nuevo movimiento conservador conocido como la Nueva Derecha. En 1980, la Nueva Derecha eligió como presidente a Ronald Reagan y alteró el equilibrio entre los partidos en el Congreso.

El presidente Reagan llevó a Estados Unidos en una dirección diferente de las administraciones anteriores. Como la mayoría de los conservadores, Reagan favoreció la participación limitada del gobierno en la economía. Urgió al Congreso a cortar impuestos, a reducir el gasto en programas sociales y a eliminar la reglamentación de las industrias de la banca, telecomunicaciones y de las aerolíneas. Al mismo tiempo, Reagan tomó una posición agresiva hacia la Guerra Fría. Él forzó al Congreso a aprobar grandes aumentos en el gasto militar y se comprometió en un desarrollo del aparato militar. Desgraciadamente, el aumento en estos gastos no se equilibró con los recortes a los impuestos, y el déficit fiscal y la deuda nacional se dispararon. Aunque no hubo crecimiento económico, la diferencia entre los ricos y los pobres se amplió, y el desempleo creció entre los agricultores y los obreros.

A través del final de la década de 1980, Estados Unidos se involucró en conflictos en América Latina y Asia, una participación que continuaría en el siguiente siglo. Cuando el bloque comunista de la Unión Soviética y de Europa oriental colapsó al final de la década, la gente alrededor del mundo celebró lo que consideraban un nuevo nacimiento de la democracia. Estados Unidos se convirtió en la única superpotencia. Como tal, la nación y sus líderes conservadores y liberales heredaron un nuevo grupo de retos económicos, políticos y militares.

En las próximas semanas, es posible que su estudiante quiera compartir con usted lo que ha aprendido. Por favor participe en la experiencia educativa de su hijo o hija a través de conversaciones e involucrándose en su trabajo.

Atentamente,

THE CONSERVATIVE RESURGENCE 1980–1993

1. The Conservative Movement Grows

Pacing
2 periods
1 block

L1 Special Needs
L2 Basic to Average
L3 All Students
L4 Average to Advanced

Section Objectives

- Describe the differences between liberal and conservative viewpoints.
- Analyze the reasons behind the rise of conservatism in the early 1980s.
- Explain why Ronald Reagan won the presidency in 1980.

Terms and People • liberal • conservative • New Right • unfunded mandate • Moral Majority • Ronald Reagan

Focus Question: What spurred the rise of conservatism in the late 1970s and early 1980s?

PREPARE TO READ

Build Background Knowledge
Preview the section, and remind students that the United States experienced many economic problems in the late 1970s.

Set a Purpose
Have students discuss the Witness History Selection. Point out the Section Focus Question, and have students fill in the Note Taking graphic organizer.

Preview Key Terms
Preview the section's Key Terms.

Instructional Resources
❏ **WITNESS HISTORY** Audio CD

❏ **All in One Teaching Resources**
  L3 Preread the Chapter, p. 8
  L3 Analyze Visuals, p. 10
  L3 Vocabulary Builder, p. 11
  L3 Reading Strategy, p. 12

❏ **Reading and Note Taking Study Guide**
(On-Level, Adapted, and Spanish)
Section 1

TEACH

Two Views: Liberal and Conservative
Contrast the ideologies of liberals and conservatives.

The Conservative Movement Gains Strength
Explain how the New Right rose to power in the late 1970s and early 1980s.

Reagan Wins the Presidency
Discuss the factors that led to Reagan's election in 1980.

Instructional Resources

❏ **All in One Teaching Resources**
  L3 Viewpoints: Liberals and Conservatives, p. 15

❏ **Color Transparencies**
  L3 Winning the South

❏ **Note Taking Transparencies**, B-145

ASSESS/RETEACH

Assess Progress
Evaluate student comprehension with the Section Assessment and Section Quiz.

Reteach
Assign the Reading and Note Taking Study Guide to help struggling students.

Extend
Have students use a "conservative" or a "liberal" approach to address a particular problem such as health care, poverty, or foreign affairs.

Instructional Resources

❏ **All in One Teaching Resources**
  L3 Section Quiz, p. 21

❏ **Reading and Note Taking Study Guide**
(On-Level, Adapted, and Spanish)
Section 1 Summary

❏ **Progress Monitoring Transparencies**, 141

Audio support is available for this section.
Modify lesson with notes found on the bottom of the Teacher's Edition.

THE CONSERVATIVE RESURGENCE 1980–1993

2. The Reagan Revolution

Pacing
2 periods
1 block

L1	Special Needs
L2	Basic to Average
L3	All Students
L4	Average to Advanced

Section Objectives

■ Analyze Reagan's economic policies as President.

■ Summarize how Reagan strengthened the conservative movement.

■ Evaluate the steps taken to address various problems in the 1980s and early 1990s.

Terms and People • supply-side economics • deregulation • budget deficit • national debt • Savings and Loan crisis • voucher • AIDS

Focus Question: What were the major characteristics of the conservative Reagan Revolution?

PREPARE TO READ

Build Background Knowledge
Preview the section, and remind students that conservatives favored limited government intervention in the economy.

Set a Purpose
Have students discuss the Witness History Selection. Point out the Section Focus Question, and have students fill in the Note Taking graphic organizer.

Preview Key Terms
Preview the section's Key Terms.

Instructional Resources
❏ **WITNESS HISTORY** Audio CD
❏ **Reading and Note Taking Study Guide**
(On-Level, Adapted, and Spanish)
Section 2

TEACH

Reaganomics Guides the Economy
Explain how Reagan applied supply-side economics to his economic policies.

Conservative Strength Grows
Discuss Reagan's reelection and the growth of conservatism on the Supreme Court.

Confronting Challenging Issues
Explain the ways in which Reagan addressed domestic issues.

Instructional Resources
❏ **All in One Teaching Resources**
L3 Reading a Chart: Social Security, p. 16
❏ **Skills Handbook**
L3 Giving an Oral or a Multimedia Presentation, p. 36
❏ **Color Transparencies**
L3 Reagan's Foreign Policy
❏ **Note Taking Transparencies,** B-146

ASSESS/RETEACH

Assess Progress
Evaluate student comprehension with the Section Assessment and Section Quiz.

Reteach
Assign the Reading and Note Taking Study Guide to help struggling students.

Extend
Have students debate the effectiveness of applying Reaganomics to their local economy.

Instructional Resources
❏ **All in One Teaching Resources**
L4 Enrichment: Connection to Economics, p. 13
L3 Section Quiz, p. 22
❏ **Reading and Note Taking Study Guide**
(On-Level, Adapted, and Spanish)
Section 2 Summary
❏ **Progress Monitoring Transparencies,** 142

Audio support is available for this section.
Modify lesson with notes found on the bottom of the Teacher's Edition.

THE CONSERVATIVE RESURGENCE 1980–1993

3. The End of the Cold War

Pacing
2 periods
1 block

L1 Special Needs
L2 Basic to Average
L3 All Students
L4 Average to Advanced

Section Objectives

■ Analyze the ways that Ronald Reagan challenged communism and the Soviet Union.

■ Explain why communism collapsed in Europe and in the Soviet Union.

■ Describe other foreign policy challenges that faced the United States in the 1980s.

Terms and People • SDI • Contras • Mikhail Gorbachev • *glasnost* • *perestroika* • Iran-Contra affair

Focus Question: What were Reagan's foreign policies, and how did they contribute to the fall of communism in Europe?

PREPARE TO READ

Build Background Knowledge
Preview the section, and point out that defense spending increased sharply under Reagan.

Set a Purpose
Have students discuss the Witness History Selection. Point out the Section Focus Question, and have students fill in the Note Taking graphic organizer.

Preview Key Terms
Preview the section's Key Terms.

Instructional Resources
❑ **WITNESS HISTORY** Audio CD
❑ **Reading and Note Taking Study Guide**
(On-Level, Adapted, and Spanish)
Section 3

TEACH

Reagan Challenges Communism
Discuss the approach that Reagan took toward the Soviet Union and the spread of communism.

The Cold War Ends
Explain how the communist governments in Eastern Europe and the Soviet Union collapsed.

Trouble Persists in the Middle East
Discuss the significance of the Iran-Contra affair.

Instructional Resources
❑ **All in One Teaching Resources**
L1 L2 Primary Source: *Tear Down This Wall*, p. 17
L3 Primary Source: Understanding Reagan's *Tear Down This Wall* Speech, p. 18
L3 Reading a Chart: Military Spending, p. 19
❑ **Color Transparencies**
L3 The End of Communism
❑ **Note Taking Transparencies,** B-147a, B-147b

ASSESS/RETEACH

Assess Progress
Evaluate student comprehension with the Section Assessment and Section Quiz.

Reteach
Assign the Reading and Note Taking Study Guide to help struggling students.

Extend
Extend the lesson by having students complete the online activity on the Berlin Wall.

Instructional Resources
❑ **All in One Teaching Resources**
L3 Section Quiz, p. 23
❑ **Reading and Note Taking Study Guide**
(On-Level, Adapted, and Spanish)
Section 3 Summary
❑ **Progress Monitoring Transparencies,** 143

Audio support is available for this section.
Modify lesson with notes found on the bottom of the Teacher's Edition.

THE CONSERVATIVE RESURGENCE 1980–1993

4. Foreign Policy After the Cold War

Pacing
2 periods
1 block

L1	Special Needs
L2	Basic to Average
L3	All Students
L4	Average to Advanced

Section Objectives

- Analyze why George H.W. Bush decided to use force in some foreign disputes and not in others.
- Summarize the Persian Gulf War and its results.

Terms and People • Manuel Noriega • Tiananmen Square • apartheid • Nelson Mandela • divest • Saddam Hussein • Operation Desert Storm

Focus Question: What actions did the United States take abroad during George H.W. Bush's presidency?

PREPARE TO READ

Build Background Knowledge
Preview the section, and explain that the Cold War ended during George H.W. Bush's first years in office.

Set a Purpose
Have students discuss the Witness History Selection. Point out the Section Focus Question, and have students fill in the Note Taking graphic organizer.

Preview Key Terms
Preview the section's Key Terms.

Instructional Resources
❏ **WITNESS HISTORY** Audio CD
❏ **Reading and Note Taking Study Guide** (On-Level, Adapted, and Spanish) Section 4

TEACH

A New Role in the World
Discuss the response of the United States to world events in the late 1980s and early 1990s.

The Persian Gulf War
Explain the causes, the conduct, and the outcomes of the Persian Gulf War.

Instructional Resources
❏ **All in One Teaching Resources**
  L3 Outline Map: World Oil Reserves, p. 20
❏ **Color Transparencies**
  L3 Tiananmen Square Protests
❏ **Note Taking Transparencies,** B-148

ASSESS/RETEACH

Assess Progress
Evaluate student comprehension with the Section Assessment and Section Quiz.

Reteach
Assign the Reading and Note Taking Study Guide to help struggling students.

Extend
Have students present a report about the democratic protests in China, the end of apartheid in South Africa, or the disintegration of Yugoslavia.

Instructional Resources
❏ **All in One Teaching Resources**
  L3 Section Quiz, p. 24
  L1 L2 Chapter Test A, p. 25
  L3 Chapter Test B, p. 28
❏ **Reading and Note Taking Study Guide** (On-Level, Adapted, and Spanish) Section 4 Summary
❏ **Progress Monitoring Transparencies,** 144

Audio support is available for this section.
Modify lesson with notes found on the bottom of the Teacher's Edition.

THE CONSERVATIVE RESURGENCE
Preread the Chapter: Why and How?

What is **Prereading?** It is a reading comprehension strategy. This graphic organizer aids you in prereading this chapter.

Checklist: *Place a check on the line when you have completed the following:*

_____ Read all items in the Chapter Opener.

_____ Read the titles of the charts, graphs, maps, and timeline in the Quick Study Guide and Concept Connector Cumulative Review.

_____ Read the chapter assessment.

Before you read each section of your text, look at the following material. (Chapters may have 3, 4, or 5 sections.) Check the sections as you complete the review.

Sections: 1_____ 2_____ 3_____ 4_____ 5_____ Read the Focus Question, the section opener information in the side column, and each boldface heading and subheading.

Sections: 1_____ 2_____ 3_____ 4_____ 5_____ Looked over all words that are underlined or in boldface type.

Sections: 1_____ 2_____ 3_____ 4_____ 5_____ Read all review questions within the section.

Complete the following:

1. Chapter title: _____

2. Write the main idea of each section based on its Focus Question.

Section 1: _____

_____

Section 2: _____

_____

Section 3: _____

_____

Section 4: _____

_____

Section 5: _____

_____

Preread the Chapter: Why and How? (Continued)

3. List three visual aids included in the chapter (e.g., pictures, maps, charts, diagrams, features). Describe how they will aid your understanding of the chapter.

(1) _____

_____

(2) _____

_____

(3) _____

_____

4. Describe one new or important idea you learned from reading the Quick Study Guide.

_____

_____

5. Identify two unfamiliar words that you noticed during your prereading, and determine from the context what you think the new word means.

Word #1 _____ Part of Speech _____

Clues to meaning _____

Predicted meaning _____

Word #2 _____ Part of Speech _____

Clues to meaning _____

Predicted meaning _____

6. After previewing this chapter, were you able to understand what the chapter is about?

Not understood _____ Somewhat understood _____ Easily understood _____

7. Copy the heading (titles in blue print) that you predict will be the most difficult to understand.

_____

_____

8. How many pages are in the chapter? _____

9. Estimate the time it will take you to read the chapter. _____

Analyze Visuals

Images are an effective way to communicate information. There are many types of visuals, such as photographs, paintings, and Infographics. Visuals tell a story in a dramatic or vivid style. Just as with any primary or secondary source, it is important to look closely and ask questions to determine the meaning and reliability of the visual.

Use this outline to help you better understand ideas or events conveyed by a visual. Answer these questions to the best of your ability.

Title of visual Page

1. What is the topic of the visual (what is happening)?

   _____

2. Focus on the details and list three that you find in the visual. How does each help convey information about the topic?

   _____

   _____

   _____

3. Assume you are one of the individuals in the picture, or that you were present when the image was made.

   (a) Describe who you are.

   _____

   (b) Explain what your reaction might have been to the situation.

   _____

   _____

4. The creator often reveals a bias about the subject or an attempt to get a response from the viewer. Is there anything you see in the image that tells the creator's point of view?

   _____

   _____

5. Write your own caption for the image.

   _____

THE CONSERVATIVE RESURGENCE

Vocabulary Builder

Understand Word Origins

As you learn new vocabulary, you may find it useful to look up a word's definition and origins in the dictionary. Most modern words descend, or come, from words in older languages such as Latin and Greek. Often, a word may have descended from a chain of older words. Learning a word's origins can help you better understand and use the word. The example provides the origins of the word *degeneration.*

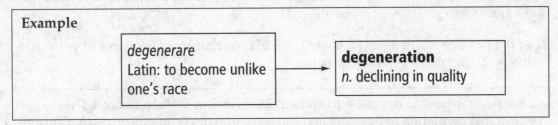

Example

degenerare
Latin: to become unlike
one's race

→ **degeneration**
n. declining in quality

Directions: *Refer to your textbook to record the meaning for each word listed below. Then, use a dictionary to record the word origins for each word listed. If a term includes more than one word origin, then list the most recent word origin that is defined. Some word entries may refer you to check a related word for the word origins.*

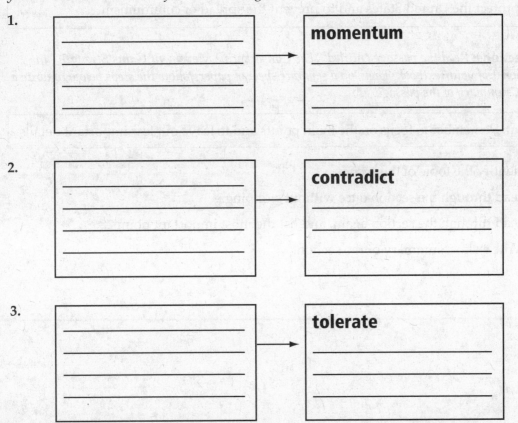

1. → **momentum**

2. → **contradict**

3. → **tolerate**

THE CONSERVATIVE RESURGENCE

Reading Strategy

Summarize

As you study history, you should learn to summarize the texts that you read. Summarizing will help you recall important information and make connections between key events and ideas. To summarize a section of text, you write a short statement recalling the most important information. You may find it useful to read a section through once and then to go back and make notes as you read the section a second time. Then, you can organize the important points from your notes into a summary.

Read the passage entitled *The Ideas and Goals of Conservatism* in Section 1 of your textbook. Then, read the summary below.

> Conservatives tend to oppose government intervention in the economy. They believe that regulation of business and industry impairs economic growth. Conservatives also worry about the erosion of traditional Christian values in society, and work to promote their religious beliefs, especially as they apply to the family. For many years, anticommunism formed the basis of modern conservative thought, and conservatives emphasized the importance of a strong national defense system to protect the United States and to prevent the spread of communism.

Directions: *Read the passage entitled "The Conservative Movement Gains Strength" in Section 1 of your textbook. Then, on a separate sheet of paper, follow the steps below to write a short summary of the passage.*

> **Hint:** Remember to focus on the main points and to leave out less important details.

1. Identify the topic of the section.

2. Read through the section once without stopping.

3. Read through the section again, and list the most important points.

4. Write a short summary of the section.

Enrichment: Connection to Economics

Reaganomics

During the 1980s, President Ronald Reagan urged Congress to pass laws based on supply-side economics. The term *supply-side economics* comes from the economic theory of supply and demand in a free market system: business and industry produce the supply to meet the demand of consumers. The free market, or capitalist, system relies on the assumption that the forces of supply and demand fluctuate continually to balance each other. Supporters of supply-side economics emphasize the need for unregulated production to generate economic growth. Supply-siders also advocate low taxes to provide workers with incentives to work, because more of the money they make goes into their pockets. The work they do produces more, and the money they earn enables them to spend more, which, in turn, encourages more production. Reaganomics, like traditional supply-side economics, focused on cutting taxes and increasing production. Like many economic policies, Reaganomics had both negative and positive consequences.

Your assignment: Research and debate the effectiveness of cutting taxes to stimulate economic activity in your community: Would tax cuts help or hurt the people and businesses in your town, county, or city?

Suggested materials: note cards for recording research and organizing debate points; slides or transparencies of relevant economic data, including graphs and charts that illustrate your points; dry-erase board and markers to detail key points in the debate

Suggested Procedure

1. Organize into two groups, and decide who will debate each side of the issue.

2. Determine the rules for the debate—speaking order, time limits, and so on.

3. In groups, decide what kinds of information you need to research to make an effective argument. Read the questions on the following page for research ideas.

4. Conduct your research. Review current business and economics journals and the business sections of newspapers to learn about the current economic situation and to learn more about tax theories. Read the opinions of economists and local politicians and community leaders who both support and oppose tax cuts. Look for evidence such as statistics, charts, and graphs to support your side of the issue and to refute arguments that your opponent might make. Consider interviewing local officials to get more insight into the issue.

5. Arrange your arguments and evidence into talking points. Then, anticipate your opponent's arguments, and prepare rebuttals.

6. Write your talking points and counterarguments on note cards. Then practice for the debate by reading over your note cards several times to become familiar with them.

7. After the debate, use the chart on the following page to recall important points supporting and opposing tax cuts. Then, form an opinion about whether tax cuts would benefit your community.

Name _____ Class _____ Date _____

Enrichment: Connection to Economics

Reaganomics

Directions: *Consider the following questions as you research your side of the debate. Make sure that you base your answers to these questions on factual information.*

- What are major arguments in favor of tax cuts?

- What are major arguments against tax cuts?

- How are taxes collected at the local, state, and federal levels?

- How is money from taxes distributed and used in your community?

- What percentage of their incomes do people at different income levels pay in taxes?

- What people, services, and agencies depend on funding from taxes?

- How do taxes affect local small businesses?

- How have tax cuts and tax hikes affected economic activity in the past?

Directions: *Use the following chart to record important points made during the debate. Refer to the information that you record to form an opinion.*

Income tax cuts would help the local economy.	Income tax cuts would hurt the local economy.

Viewpoints

Liberals and conservatives in the United States hold very different opinions on matters of economic and social policy. Although both groups support the ideas of democratic government and constitutional law, they differ in their interpretation of the fundamental purposes of the government. Liberals tend to believe that government has an obligation to improve the lives of all of its citizens. Conservatives tend to believe that government has the responsibility of maintaining order so that people can work to improve their own lives. In economics, these different approaches manifest themselves in the ways that liberals and conservatives approach taxes, spending, and regulation. ◆ *As you read, consider how the opinions in these political statements differ on specific issues. Then, on a separate sheet of paper, answer the questions that follow.*

Liberals and Conservatives

Preamble from the Republican Party Platform, August 17, 1976

"The Platform is the Party's contract with the people." This is what it says on the cover of the official printing of the Democrat Platform. So it should be. The Democrats' Platform repeats the same thing on every page: more government, more spending, more inflation. Compare. This Republican Platform says exactly the opposite—less government, less spending, less inflation. In other words, we want you to retain more of your own money, money that represents the worth of your labors, to use as you see fit for the necessities and conveniences of life.

No matter how many statements to the contrary that Mr. Carter makes, he is firmly attached to a contract with you to increase vastly the powers of government. Is bigger government in Washington really what you want?

Source: Available online at http://www.ford.utexas.edu/library/document/platform/preamble.htm.

Speech to Citizens Organized Acting Together (COACT), 1981, by Paul Wellsone

This Administration tells us we must sacrifice so we can once again have a strong economy. So we see $48.6 billion in social spending cuts—cuts in legal services, health care, food assistance, energy assistance, job training, education, medical, social security. This scorched-earth budget cutting deserves to be called exactly what it is—a class war against the poor and oppressed. . . . It is a program of meanness—one that we will not accept.

This Administration is getting the government off our back so the corporations and the military defense establishment can jump on. Meanwhile, schools, health care, jobs, assistance to poor people and local services to citizens are cut severely as part of the attack on government. Yet the biggest part of the government by far is the Pentagon, and its budget grows by leaps and bounds.

Source: Available online at http://www.wellstone.org/archive/article_detail.aspx?itemlóD=5421&catID=3605.

Questions to Think About

1. What does the Republican Party Platform say that "less government, less spending" will mean for people?

2. With what does Paul Wellstone say the Reagan administration wants to replace government control?

3. **Detect Points of View** Which statement reflects conservative thought? Which reflects liberal thought? Explain your answer.

4. **Draw Conclusions** Why do you think Wellstone refers to the administration's budget cuts as class warfare?

Reading a Chart

During Ronald Reagan's presidency, the Republican Congress made significant changes to the Social Security system. The costs of Social Security had gone up dramatically as more people enrolled in the program. Better healthcare, nutrition, and sanitation also meant that more people were living longer and collecting more benefits. Congress enacted the Social Security Reform Act of 1983 to prevent the system from running out of money. The ability of Social Security to keep up with the needs of retirees continues to concern people today. ◆ *Study the chart below. Then, on a separate sheet of paper, answer the questions that follow.*

Social Security

	Before 1983	After 1983
Social Security covers new federal employees, most current employees of the legislative branch, all members of Congress, the President and Vice President, federal judges, and other executive-level political appointees.	No	Yes
Social Security covers employees of tax-exempt nonprofit organizations.	No	Yes
States can terminate Social Security coverage for state and local employees.	Yes	No
Disabled widow(er)s, disabled surviving divorced spouses, and surviving divorced spouses who remarry remain eligible for Social Security benefits.	No	Yes
Tax rates for employers and employees are 7 percent or higher. (Rates increased to 7.65 percent in 1990.)	No	Yes
A portion of Social Security income is taxable for recipients with income above specified levels.	No	Yes
Retirement age is above 65.	No	Yes

Questions to Think About

1. Who gained coverage under the Social Security Reform Act of 1983?

2. What happened to tax rates for Social Security in 1983?

3. **Clarify Problems** How was the Social Security Reform Act meant to ensure that the Social Security system would not run out of money?

4. **Link Past to Present** Today, politicians continue to discuss reforming the Social Security system to avoid a financial crisis. What problems with Social Security that existed in 1983 do you think exist today?

Primary Source

In 1987, President Ronald Reagan gave a speech in West Berlin in which he appealed to Mikhail Gorbachev to tear down the wall that divided the German people. The East German government had built the wall in 1961 to prevent East Germans from escaping into West Germany through West Berlin. The wall surrounded West Berlin with 103 miles of concrete. More than 10,000 people tried to cross it, but only about half of them succeeded. ◆ *As you read, think about what the Berlin Wall meant to the people of Eastern and Western Europe. Then, on a separate sheet of paper, answer the questions below.*

Tear Down This Wall

We hear much from Moscow about a new policy of reform and openness. Some political prisoners have been released. Certain foreign news broadcasts are no longer being jammed [blocked]. Some economic enterprises [businesses] have been permitted [allowed] to operate with greater freedom from state control.

Are these the beginnings of profound [major] changes in the Soviet state? Or are they token gestures, intended to raise false hopes in the West, or to strengthen the Soviet system without changing it? We welcome change and openness; for we believe that freedom and security go together, that the advance of human liberty can only strengthen the cause of world peace. There is one sign the Soviets can make that would be unmistakable, that would advance dramatically the cause of freedom and peace.

General Secretary Gorbachev, if you seek [are looking for] peace, if you seek prosperity [wealth] for the Soviet Union and Eastern Europe, if you seek liberalization [freedom]: Come here to this gate! Mr. Gorbachev, open this gate! Mr. Gorbachev, tear down this wall!

Source: "Tear Down This Wall: Remarks at the Brandenburg Gate," Ronald Reagan, June 12, 1987, from the Ronald Reagan Presidential Library. Available online at http://www.reaganfoundation.org/reagan/speeches/wall.asp.

Questions to Think About

1. What does President Reagan mean when he says that "certain foreign news broadcasts are no longer being jammed"?

2. What other signs of reform and openness in the Soviet Union does Reagan note?

3. What does Reagan say that Gorbachev could do to prove his commitment to peace and freedom?

4. **Draw Conclusions** Why would this action confirm Gorbachev's commitment to reform?

THE CONSERVATIVE RESURGENCE

Primary Source

In 1987, President Ronald Reagan gave a speech in West Berlin in which he appealed to Mikhail Gorbachev to make his reform efforts meaningful by tearing down the wall that divided the German people. The East German government had erected the wall in 1961 to prevent East Germans from escaping into West Germany through West Berlin. The wall encircled West Berlin in 103 miles of concrete. More than 10,000 people had tried to cross it, but only about half of them had succeeded. ◆ *As you read, think about what the Berlin Wall symbolized for the people of Eastern and Western Europe. Then, on a separate sheet of paper, answer the questions below.*

Understanding Reagan's *Tear Down This Wall* Speech

Behind me stands a wall that encircles the free sectors of this city, part of a vast system of barriers that divides the entire continent of Europe. From the Baltic, south, those barriers cut across Germany in a gash of barbed wire, concrete, dog runs, and guard towers. Farther south, there may be no visible, no obvious wall. But there remain armed guards and checkpoints all the same—still a restriction on the right to travel, still an instrument to impose upon ordinary men and women the will of a totalitarian state. . . .

Today I say: As long as the gate is closed, as long as this scar of a wall is permitted to stand, it is not the German question alone that remains open, but the question of freedom for all mankind. . . .

We hear much from Moscow about a new policy of reform and openness. Some political prisoners have been released. Certain foreign news broadcasts are no longer being jammed. Some economic enterprises have been permitted to operate with greater freedom from state control.

Are these the beginnings of profound changes in the Soviet state? Or are they token gestures, intended to raise false hopes in the West, or to strengthen the Soviet system without changing it? We welcome change and openness; for we believe that freedom and security go together, that the advance of human liberty can only strengthen the cause of world peace. There is one sign the Soviets can make that would be unmistakable, that would advance dramatically the cause of freedom and peace.

General Secretary Gorbachev, if you seek peace, if you seek prosperity for the Soviet Union and Eastern Europe, if you seek liberalization: Come here to this gate! Mr. Gorbachev, open this gate! Mr. Gorbachev, tear down this wall!

Source: "Tear Down This Wall: Remarks at the Brandenburg Gate," Ronald Reagan, June 12, 1987, from the Ronald Reagan Presidential Library. Available online at http://www.reaganfoundation.org/reagan/speeches/wall.asp.

Questions to Think About

1. Of what does Reagan say that the Berlin Wall is part?

2. What signs does Reagan see that the Soviet Union is reforming?

3. **Draw Conclusions** Why does Reagan say that, as long as the wall is allowed to stand, the question of freedom for all humanity remains open?

4. **Activity** In this speech, Reagan asks Gorbachev to tear down the Berlin Wall to prove his commitment to reform. On a separate sheet of paper, list actions that citizens today can take to demonstrate their commitment to democracy. Then, list actions that world leaders can take to demonstrate their commitment to democracy.

THE CONSERVATIVE RESURGENCE

Reading a Chart

Military Spending

President Ronald Reagan opposed big government and worked to cut taxes and reduce government spending on social programs. At the same time, however, Reagan urged Congress to increase defense and military spending. Reagan believed that the United States had to engage in a massive arms buildup in order to tip the balance of power between the United States and the Soviet Union. He also engaged U.S. troops, arms, and funds in nations around the globe in order to prevent the spread of communism and to maintain American influence. ◆ *Study the chart below and the chart entitled Federal Defense Spending, 1978–1990, in Section 3 of your textbook. Then, on a separate sheet of paper, answer the questions that follow.*

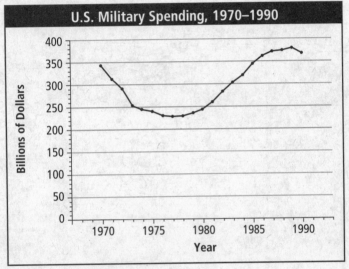

Source: Center for Defense Information

Questions to Think About

1. Approximately how much did the federal government spend on the military the year before Reagan became President?

2. In what year did both military and defense spending peak?

3. **Interpret Charts** What do the data in both charts tell you about military and defense spending during President Reagan's administration?

4. **Draw Conclusions** Why do you think military spending decreased steadily in the early 1970s?

Outline Map

World Oil Reserves

Directions: *Use the data below to locate and shade the fifteen nations that possess the largest known oil reserves. Shade the countries as follows: red for more than 200 billion barrels, orange for more than 100 billion barrels, yellow for more than 50 billion barrels, green for more than 25 billion barrels, and blue for more than 15 billion barrels. Fill in the key to reflect this shading scheme. You may use any map in the textbook chapter, unit opener, or Atlas for reference.*

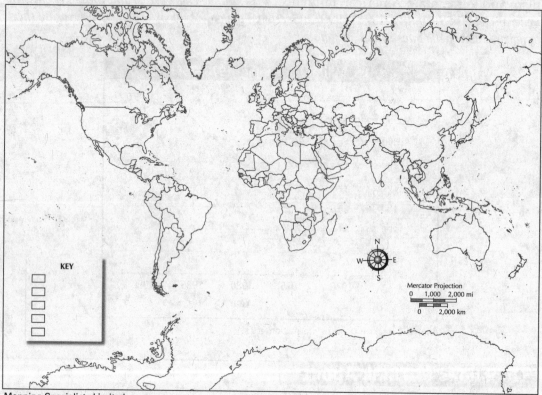

Mapping Specialists Limited

Nation	Amount (billions of barrels)	Nation	Amount (billions of barrels)
Saudi Arabia	262.7	Libya	40.0
Canada	178.9	Nigeria	36.0
Iran	133.3	Mexico	33.3
Iraq	112.5	Kazakhstan	26.0
United Arab Emirates	97.8	Angola	25.0
Kuwait	96.5	United States	22.5
Venezuela	75.6	China	18.3
Russia	69.0		

THE CONSERVATIVE RESURGENCE
Section 1 Quiz

A. Key Terms and People

Directions: *Match each term or person in Column II with the correct definition in Column I.*

Column I

_____ 1. a program required but not paid for by the federal government

_____ 2. politicians who generally favor government intervention in the economy to address inequalities

_____ 3. a political organization founded by Reverend Jerry Falwell to fulfill religious goals

_____ 4. politicians who generally favor limited government intervention in the economy

_____ 5. a resurgent conservative movement that grew rapidly during the 1960s and 1970s

_____ 6. conservative president elected in 1980

Column II

a. liberals
b. conservatives
c. New Right
d. unfunded mandate
e. Moral Majority
f. Ronald Reagan

B. Key Concepts

Directions: *Write the letter of the best answer or ending in the space provided.*

_____ 7. Liberals tend to prefer which of the following in foreign policy?
   a. isolation
   b. international cooperation
   c. unilateral action
   d. limited global involvement

_____ 8. Some conservatives believe that a large central government
   a. harms economic growth.
   b. promotes industrialization.
   c. undermines public welfare.
   d. encourages individual choice.

_____ 9. Neoconservatives warn about the dangers posed to society by
   a. inhibiting the mass media.
   b. funding religious programs.
   c. abandoning traditional values.
   d. resisting the counterculture.

_____ 10. Ronald Reagan convinced many Americans that he would
   a. usher in a new era of prosperity.
   b. end the Cold War with the Soviet Union.
   c. use higher taxes to increase the public welfare.
   d. focus on practical action rather than on idealistic optimism.

THE CONSERVATIVE RESURGENCE

Section 2 Quiz

A. Key Terms and People

Directions: *Use the terms in the word bank to complete the statements below. You will not use all of the terms.*

supply-side economics	deregulation	budget deficit	national debt
Savings and Loan crisis	vouchers	AIDS	

1. The Reagan administration presided over the _____ of the airline, telecommunications, and banking industries.

2. Liberals argued that _____ took money away from public schools.

3. Reagan reduced taxes but increased defense spending, causing a _____.

4. The theory of _____ rested on the idea that lower taxes would encourage people to work more so that they would have more money to spend.

5. The amount of money owed by the federal government, or the _____, skyrocketed during Reagan's presidency.

6. The _____ resulted from fraudulent business activity and risky lending.

B. Key Concepts

Directions: *Write the letter of the best answer or ending in the space provided.*

_____ 7. "Reaganomics" emphasized
   a. tax cuts.   c. defense reductions.
   b. social spending.   d. regulation of industry.

_____ 8. Despite an economic turn-around in 1983,
   a. inflation rose dramatically.
   b. tax rates continued to go up.
   c. the number of the working poor increased.
   d. immigration to the United States declined.

_____ 9. On what issue did Justice Sandra Day O'Connor consistently break with other conservative judges?
   a. abortion   c. religion in schools
   b. labor rights   d. Social Security reform

_____ 10. *A Nation at Risk* reported on the
   a. rising threat of AIDS.
   b. coming crisis in Social Security.
   c. declining test scores of students.
   d. income gap between the rich and the poor.

THE CONSERVATIVE RESURGENCE

Section 3 Quiz

A. Key Terms and People

Directions: *Write a definition for each term or person listed below.*

1. SDI _____

    _____

2. Contras _____

    _____

3. Mikhail Gorbachev _____

    _____

4. *glasnost* _____

    _____

5. *perestroika* _____

    _____

6. Iran-Contra affair _____

    _____

B. Key Concepts

Directions: *Write the letter of the best answer or ending in the space provided.*

_____ 7. The Reagan administration committed the United States to a

     a. massive arms buildup.   **c.** policy of nonintervention.

     b. nuclear weapons freeze.   **d.** withdrawal from the Cold War.

_____ 8. Reagan supported rebellions in Afghanistan, Nicaragua, El Salvador, and Grenada to

     a. protect human rights.   **c.** promote democratic governments.

     b. weaken the Soviet Union.   **d.** undermine right-wing extremists.

_____ 9. The START I treaty aimed to

     a. delay the Star Wars program.

     b. rebuild the former Soviet republics.

     c. end communist control of eastern Europe.

     d. reduce the number of nuclear weapons in the world.

_____ 10. Which of the following symbolized the end of communism in Europe?

     a. the fall of the Berlin Wall

     b. the collapse of the Soviet Union

     c. the destruction of a statue of Stalin

     d. the summit between Gorbachev and Reagan

THE CONSERVATIVE RESURGENCE
Section 4 Quiz

A. Key Terms and People

Directions: *Match each term or person in Column II with the correct definition in Column I. You will not use all of the terms and people.*

Column I

_____ 1. leader of the antiapartheid movement in South Africa

_____ 2. an oppressive system of rigid segregation

_____ 3. leader of Panama convicted in the United States of drug trafficking

_____ 4. an American-led attack on Iraqi forces in the Middle East

_____ 5. the scene of prodemocracy protests in which hundreds of people were killed

_____ 6. dictator of Iraq who ordered the invasion of Kuwait

Column II

a. Manuel Noriega

b. Tiananmen Square

c. apartheid

d. Nelson Mandela

e. divest

f. Saddam Hussein

g. Operation Desert Storm

B. Key Concepts

Directions: *Write the letter of the best answer or ending in the space provided.*

_____ 7. The Bush administration cracked down on drug trafficking from
    a. Africa.   c. Latin America.
    b. China.   d. the Middle East.

_____ 8. Congress pressured South Africa to change its apartheid system by
    a. suspending arms sales.   c. withdrawing all investments.
    b. severing diplomatic ties.   d. imposing economic sanctions.

_____ 9. Bush launched "Operation Restore Hope" to protect human rights in
    a. China.   c. South Africa.
    b. Somalia.   d. Yugoslavia.

_____ 10. Which of the following best describes the 1991 Persian Gulf War?
    a. short, with few casualties
    b. short, with few American casualties
    c. long, with few American casualties
    d. long, with many casualties

THE CONSERVATIVE RESURGENCE

Test A

A. Key Terms and People

Directions: *Match each term or person in Column II with the correct definition in Column I. Write the correct letter in each blank. (3 points each)*

Column I

_____ 1. a leader of Panama seized by the United States for drug trafficking

_____ 2. a disease of the immune system that first appeared in 1981

_____ 3. programs required but not paid for by the government

_____ 4. a conservative movement that grew rapidly during the 1960s and 1970s

_____ 5. the leader of Iraq who invaded Kuwait in 1990

_____ 6. a leader of the Soviet Union who brought about many reforms

_____ 7. the first leader of South Africa elected in free elections

_____ 8. an event in which many banks failed

_____ 9. the theory that people will work more to make and spend more money if their taxes are lower

_____ 10. a program that would use lasers on land and in space to destroy missiles aimed at the United States

Column II

a. New Right

b. unfunded mandates

c. supply-side economics

d. Savings and Loan Crisis

e. AIDS

f. Mikhail Gorbachev

g. SDI

h. Manuel Noriega

i. Nelson Mandela

j. Saddam Hussein

B. Key Concepts

Directions: *Write the letter of the best answer or ending in the space provided. (4 points each)*

_____ 11. Conservatives tend to prefer helping the needy through

    a. higher minimum wage laws.

    b. government programs such as Social Security.

    c. charity provided by private organizations and individuals.

_____ 12. In the late 1970s, liberals supported

    a. deregulation of industry.

    b. tax cuts and reduced social spending.

    c. laws protecting the rights of minorities and women.

_____ 13. Conservatives gained power in the 1970s in part because

    a. liberals became more involved with religious groups.

    b. many white southerners opposed the civil rights laws of the 1960s.

    c. the counterculture drove many Middle Americans into the Democratic party.

_____ 14. According to supply-side economics, Reagan needed to cut taxes and

    a. balance the budget.   **c.** increase defense spending.

    b. cut spending on social programs.

_____ 15. Which of the following resulted from the Economic Recovery Act of 1981?

    a. Spending on social programs increased.

    b. The richest Americans received the largest tax cuts.

    c. The government increased federal regulation of industry.

_____ 16. During his election campaign in 1988, George H.W. Bush promised not to

    a. raise taxes.   **c.** engage in foreign conflicts.

    b. cut funding for welfare.

_____ 17. President Reagan's "Star Wars" program would have

    a. put weapons in space.

    b. increased nuclear weapons production.

    c. stopped any attack against the United States.

_____ 18. Why did Gorbachev pursue *glasnost* and *perestroika* reforms?

    a. The Soviet economy could not keep up with the arms race.

    b. The United States demonstrated that it had greater nuclear capacity.

    c. Russian revolutionaries staged a violent uprising.

_____ 19. In August 1991, Boris Yelstin

    a. asked for U.S. help to overthrow communist rule in the Soviet Union.

    b. rallied millions of Russians to support Gorbachev's reforms.

    c. seized control of the Soviet government and declared himself President.

Use the map below to answer question 20.

_____ 20. The Persian Gulf War in 1991 came about because F invaded which of the following?

    a. A

    b. H

    c. I

Mapping Specialists Limited

C. Document-Based Questions

Directions: *Read the passage below. Then, on the back of this paper or on a separate sheet of paper, answer the question that follows. (10 points)*

> For anyone, who didn't experience the Wall, it will be hard to imagine what an overwhelming feeling of relief, of joy, of unreality filled one that this monster was dead, and people had conquered it. The years of degrading [humiliating] searches at border crossings, the loved ones who were walled in on the eastern side. [East Germany's] restrictions, regulations, bureaucratic border formalities, the dogs and soldiers with machine guns, the main streets cut off suddenly by this cold, hard cement wall—all of this was suddenly defeated, and one could dance on its dead body or chip off a piece of it with a hammer. Just days before, either action might have meant arrest or even being shot. I tell you, it was a giddy, delirious feeling—even for someone completely sober.
>
> I moved to the eastern edge of the Wall and sat down with my feet dangling into East Berlin. I chatted with a 19-year-old East German boy from the countryside of Thuringia. He asked me to describe the skyscrapers of New York. I tried, but eventually told him: "You have to see it yourself. And now you can."
>
> —*Richard Pinard, BBC's "On This Day," November 9, 1989*

21. Synthesize Information Why does Pinard say, "And now you can"?

D. Critical Thinking and Writing

Directions: *Answer the following questions on the back of this paper or on a separate sheet of paper. (10 points each)*

22. Summarize Explain three reasons that conservatives gained political power during the 1970s.

23. Compare and Contrast During President George H.W. Bush's term in office, the United States sent troops into Panama, Yugoslavia, and Kuwait. President Bush's reasons for involvement and his actions differed in each country. Compare and contrast the decisions he made with regards to two of these countries.

THE CONSERVATIVE RESURGENCE

Test B

A. Key Terms and People

Directions: *Match the correct term or person in Column II with its definition in Column I. Write the correct letter in each blank. You will not use all of the terms and people. (3 points each)*

Column I

_____ 1. a dictator seized by the United States for drug trafficking

_____ 2. a disease that first appeared in 1981

_____ 3. programs required but not paid for by the federal government

_____ 4. a resurgent conservative movement that grew rapidly during the 1960s and 1970s

_____ 5. a dictator who invaded another country in 1990

_____ 6. a leader who brought about many political and economic reforms in his country

_____ 7. the first leader elected in free elections in his country

_____ 8. an event in which many banks failed due to fraudulent and risky activities

_____ 9. a theory based on the idea that lower taxes will encourage people to work more to earn more money to spend

_____ 10. a proposed program that would use land and space-based lasers to destroy missiles aimed at the United States

Column II

a. conservative

b. New Right

c. Moral Majority

d. unfunded mandates

e. supply-side economics

f. national debt

g. Savings and Loan crisis

h. vouchers

i. AIDS

j. SDI

k. Mikhail Gorbachev

l. Manuel Noriega

m. Nelson Mandela

n. Saddam Hussein

B. Key Concepts

Directions: *Write the letter of the best answer or ending in the space provided. (4 points each)*

_____ 11. Conservatives tend to favor which of the following?

    a. relying on private organizations and individuals to help those in need

    b. regulating business and industry to ensure a fair distribution of wealth

    c. funding government programs to provide for the general welfare

    d. raising taxes for people with higher incomes

_____ **12.** Liberals supported which of the following in the 1970s?

    a. tax cuts for the wealthy   **c.** reduced social spending

    b. deregulation of industry   **d.** civil rights laws

_____ **13.** Conservatives gained power in the 1970s in part because

    a. liberals began pursuing more policies based on religious values.

    b. economic prosperity convinced voters to stick with the party in power.

    c. the counterculture drove Middle Americans into the Democratic party.

    d. many white southerners changed party allegiance.

_____ **14.** To compensate for cutting taxes, President Reagan convinced Congress to

    a. balance the budget.   **c.** increase defense spending.

    b. cut social spending.   **d.** add government regulatory programs.

_____ **15.** Which of the following resulted from the Economic Recovery Act of 1981?

    a. Congress introduced new social welfare programs.

    b. The wealthiest Americans received the largest tax cuts.

    c. The budget deficit decreased and unemployment dropped.

    d. The government increased funding for federal regulatory agencies.

_____ **16.** During his election campaign in 1988, George H.W. Bush promised not to

    a. raise taxes.   **c.** cut welfare funding.

    b. engage in foreign conflicts.   **d.** increase the retirement age.

_____ **17.** The proposed "Star Wars" program involved

    a. putting weapons in space.

    b. selling arms to other nations.

    c. increasing nuclear weapons production.

    d. attacking the Soviet Union before it could attack the United States.

_____ **18.** Gorbachev pursued *glasnost* and *perestroika* reforms in part because

    a. the war in Afghanistan had drained the nation's resources.

    b. the Soviet Union had already demonstrated superior nuclear capability.

    c. production increases created stable economic conditions.

    d. Russian revolutionaries staged a coup to overthrow the government.

_____ **19.** Boris Yelstin became the first leader of the Russian Federation by

    a. inciting a workers' revolution.

    b. seizing control of the communist government.

    c. leading a coup against Gorbachev's government.

    d. rallying millions of Russians to support Gorbachev's reforms.

Use the map below to answer question 20.

_____ **20.** The Persian Gulf War
in 1991 came about
because the United
States wanted to

a. protect G and H
against F.

b. support F in its
war with I.

c. overthrow the
government of F.

d. secure A from attack
by E and F.

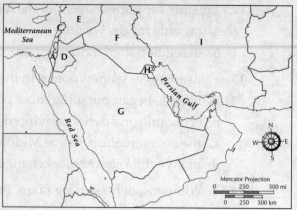

Mapping Specialists Limited

C. Document-Based Questions

Directions: *Read the passage below. Then, on the back of this paper or on a separate sheet of paper, answer the question that follows. (10 points)*

For anyone, who didn't experience the Wall, it will be hard to imagine what an overwhelming feeling of relief, of joy, of unreality filled one that this monster was dead, and people had conquered it. The years of degrading searches at border crossings, the loved ones who were walled in on the eastern side. [East Germany's] restrictions, regulations, bureaucratic border formalities, the dogs and soldiers with machine guns, the main streets cut off suddenly by this cold, hard cement wall—all of this was suddenly defeated, and one could dance on its dead body or chip off a piece of it with a hammer. Just days before, either action might have meant arrest or even being shot. I tell you, it was a giddy, delirious feeling—even for someone completely sober.

I moved to the eastern edge of the Wall and sat down with my feet dangling into East Berlin. I chatted with a 19-year-old East German boy from the country-side of Thuringia. He asked me to describe the skyscrapers of New York. I tried, but eventually told him: "You have to see it yourself. And now you can."

—*Richard Pinard, BBC's "On This Day," November 9, 1989*

21. Synthesize Information Why does Pinard say, "And now you can"?

D. Critical Thinking and Writing

Directions: *Answer the following questions on the back of this paper or on a separate sheet of paper. (10 points each)*

22. Synthesize Information Describe the growth of the conservative movement in the United States during the 1970s.

23. Compare and Contrast Discuss President George H.W. Bush's foreign policy by comparing and contrasting his decisions regarding three of the following countries: Kuwait, Panama, Somalia, and Yugoslavia. Explain why you think that he made the decisions that he made.

Answer Key

Vocabulary Builder

Student responses should demonstrate understanding of the vocabulary.

Reading Strategy

Possible response: During the 1960s and 1970s, the conservative movement gained new momentum through the New Right. The New Right gained strength as the Democratic Party lost voters. The Moral Majority, a fundamentalist religious organization, attracted new voters to the Republican Party. Changes in demographics also helped the growth of conservatism as more people from cities to suburbs and as white southern voters shifted party allegiances in response to civil rights reforms.

Enrichment

Student projects should demonstrate research, creative thinking, and appropriate presentation. Use *Assessment Rubrics* to evaluate the project.

Viewpoints
Liberals and Conservatives

1. People will be able to keep more of their own money.
2. Paul Wellstone says that the Reagan administration wants to get the government off citizens' backs so that corporations and the defense establishment can get on instead.
3. The first statement reflects conservative thought because it favors limited government, lower taxes, less spending, and less inflation. The second statement reflects a liberal way of thinking because it criticizes conservative cuts as harming social welfare.
4. Wellstone refers to the budget cuts as class warfare because they affect services most needed by poor and disadvantaged people, such as education, healthcare, and energy assistance. Wealthier people do not need such assistance.

Reading a Chart
Social Security

1. new federal employees, most current employees of the legislative branch, all members of Congress, the President and Vice President, federal judges, and other executive-level political appointees; employees of tax-exempt nonprofit organizations; disabled widow(er)s, disabled surviving divorced spouses, and surviving divorced spouses who remarry
2. They increased to 7 percent or higher.
3. The act increased the tax rate, raised the age of eligibility above 65, and made some Social Security benefits taxable.
4. Social Security is paying out more than it is taking in because more people become eligible for the program each year. People continue to live longer, so many more people are collecting benefits while an insufficient number are paying into the system.

Primary Source
Tear Down This Wall

1. Radio broadcasts from outside the Soviet Union or Eastern Europe are no longer being blocked by the government; therefore, people can listen to them.
2. Political prisoners are being released, and some businesses are being allowed to operate without state control.
3. tear down the Berlin Wall
4. The Berlin Wall was a symbol of communist control and intimidation for more than twenty years. Tearing it down would show that Gorbachev was committed to ending communism and to ending the fear and oppression that went along with it.

Answer Key

Primary Source
Understanding Reagan's
Tear Down This Wall Speech

1. Reagan says that the Berlin Wall is part of a vast system of barriers that divides the entire continent of Europe.
2. Political prisoners have been released. Certain foreign news broadcasts are no longer being blocked. Some businesses have been allowed to operate without state control.
3. The wall had been a symbol of communist oppression for more than twenty years. As long as it stood, certain people in the world were not free and other people tolerated their not being free.
4. Students' responses will vary. Possible responses for citizens include voting, writing and calling elected representatives, running for office, and engaging in nonviolent protest. Possible responses for world leaders include holding free elections, protecting the voting rights of all citizens, participating in the United Nations, guaranteeing a free press, and allowing citizens unrestricted access to the Internet and other forms of information.

Reading a Chart
Military Spending

1. approximately 240 billion dollars
2. 1989
3. Both military and defense spending rose steadily throughout Reagan's administration.
4. The United States engaged in no major conflicts during the 1970s, so defense spending continued to decline throughout the decade.

Outline Map

Students should locate the nations listed in the chart. Students should shade the nations as follows: red—Saudi Arabia; orange—Canada, Iran, Iraq; yellow—United Arab Emirates, Kuwait, Venezuela, Russia; green—Libya, Nigeria, Mexico, Kazakhstan; blue—Angola, United States, China. Students should add colors and labels to the key.

Section 1 Quiz

1. d	2. a	3. e	4. b	5. c
6. f	7. b	8. a	9. c	10. a

Section 2 Quiz

1. deregulation
2. vouchers
3. budget deficit
4. supply-side economics
5. national debt
6. Savings and Loan crisis
7. a   8. c   9. a   10. c

Section 3 Quiz

1. the Strategic Defense Initiative, a proposed program to develop land and space-based lasers to destroy missiles aimed at the United States
2. anticommunist counterrevolutionaries backed by the Reagan administration in Nicaragua
3. the leader of the Soviet Union who ushered in an era of reform based on the twin policies of *glasnost* and *perestroika*
4. a reform policy pursued by Gorbachev meaning "new openness"
5. a reform policy pursued by Gorbachev that moved the Soviet Union away from a state-controlled economy
6. incident in which the government sold weapons to one nation and used the money to fund counterrevolutionaires in another nation
7. a   8. b   9. d   10. a

Answer Key

(continued)

Section 4 Quiz

1. d	2. c	3. a	4. g	5. b
6. f	7. c	8. d	9. b	10. b

Test A

1. h	2. e	3. b	4. a	5. j
6. f	7. i	8. d	9. c	10. g
11. c	12. c	13. b	14. b	15. b
16. a	17. a	18. a	19. b	20. b

21. Before the collapse of the Berlin Wall, people in East Berlin could not leave the city or country freely. The fall of the Berlin Wall symbolized the collapse of communist rule in East Germany, which meant that East Germans would be able to travel freely again.

22. Possible responses: The Vietnam War and urban riots of the 1960s divided the Democratic party and Democratic voters. The counterculture alienated many Middle Americans and white conservative Christians in the South. Watergate, the oil crises, and the Iran hostage crisis weakened confidence in the federal government.

23. Possible responses: President Bush became involved in Panama as part of the "war on drugs." President Bush did not want to become involved in the civil war in Yugoslavia because he feared that it would escalate into another Vietnam War. President Bush responded quickly to Iraq's invasion of Kuwait to prevent Saddam Hussein from gaining control of the oil reserves of Kuwait and Saudi Arabia.

Test B

1. m	2. i	3. d	4. b	5. n
6. k	7. m	8. g	9. e	10. j
11. a	12. d	13. d	14. b	15. b
16. a	17. a	18. a	19. d	20. a

21. Before the collapse of the Berlin Wall, people in East Berlin could not leave the city or country freely. The fall of the Berlin Wall symbolized the collapse of communist rule in East Germany, which meant that East Germans would be able to travel freely again.

22. The conservative movement grew throughout the 1970s, and culminated in Republican Ronald Reagan's election as president in 1980. The New Right combined the conservative interests of several groups, and appealed to voters to reform economic policies, to promote traditional Christian values, and to fight communism. The new conservatives criticized liberal policies for causing stagflation, making unfunded mandates, and creating a welfare society that lacked accountability. Republicans also benefited when many white southerners shifted their party allegiance in response to the civil rights policies of the Democrats.

23. Possible responses: In the late 1980s, President Bush focused on fighting a "war on drugs" in Latin America because he believed that drug trafficking threatened the nation's security. In 1989, President Bush sent 12,000 troops into Panama to arrest its leader, Manuel Noriega, and bring him back to the United States for trial on drug trafficking charges. In contrast, President Bush tried to avoid involving the United States in the civil war in Yugoslavia because he feared that it would escalate into another Vietnam War, and the conflict did not directly affect U.S. security. When Bush finally involved the United States, he did so as part of a UN plan to restore peace in Bosnia, one of the former Yugoslav republics. President Bush intervened more quickly—but in a similar peacekeeping capacity—in Somalia by sending Marines to establish a ceasefire and to deliver food to starving Somalis. Bush may have intervened more quickly in Somalia than in Yugoslavia because he thought the United States could better contain the conflict.